POLITICAL PROFILES
MICHELLE OBAMA

Political Profiles
Michelle Obama

Jeff C. Young

MORGAN REYNOLDS

PUBLISHING

Greensboro, North Carolina

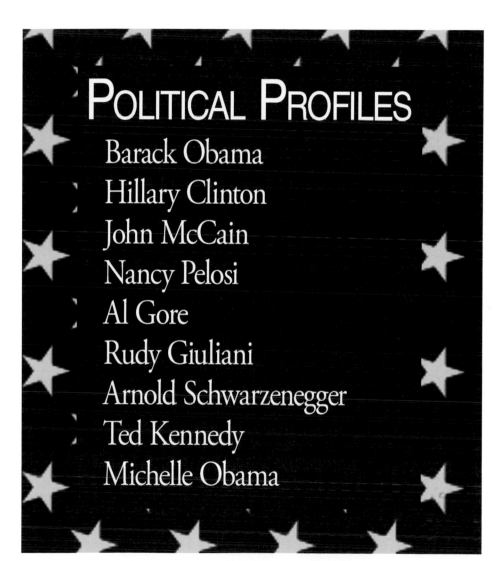

POLITICAL PROFILES

Barack Obama
Hillary Clinton
John McCain
Nancy Pelosi
Al Gore
Rudy Giuliani
Arnold Schwarzenegger
Ted Kennedy
Michelle Obama

POLITICAL PROFILES: MICHELLE OBAMA

Copyright © 2009 By Jeff C. Young

Library of Congress
Young, Jeff C., 1948-
  Political Profiles: Michelle Obama / by Jeff C. Young.
    p. cm. -- (Political profiles)
  Includes bibliographical references and index.
  ISBN-13: 978-1-59935-090-5
  ISBN-10: 1-59935-090-4
  1. Obama, Michelle, 1964---Juvenile literature. 2. Women lawyers--
United States--Biography--Juvenile literature. 3. African American women
lawyers--Biography--Juvenile literature. 4. Legislators' spouses--United States-
-Biography--Juvenile literature. 5. Chicago (Ill.)--Biography--Juvenile litera-
ture 6. Obama, Barack--Juvenile literature. I. Title.
    E901.1.O24Y68 2009
    328.73092--dc22
    [B]

OBAMA 2008045660

Printed in the United States of America

First Edition

To Crispus Attucks, c. 1723-1770, a true American patriot

Contents

Michelle Obama
(Courtesy of AP Images)

one

From the South Side to Harvard

A s a young girl, Michelle Robinson tagged along with her father as he went door to door, registering the people in their neighborhood to vote. He volunteered as the precinct captain for the Democratic Party in his South Side Chicago neighborhood, and made sure that on election days, people got to the voting booths.

"My father loved educating folks about their rights, and he believed deeply in the responsibilities that come with being participants in our rich and varied society," Michelle said later. "He never missed an opportunity to vote. He viewed it as a moral obligation."

The value of voting and of being an active participant in society was instilled in Michelle. It would be vital to her career, in which she worked tirelessly to help her community and inspire others to volunteer and do the same. And it

A skyline view of Chicago, Illinois, where Michelle lived most of her life.

would be central to her when she began supporting her husband, Barack Obama, in his quest to become president of the United States. She said, "When we vote, we don't just choose a candidate. We choose to begin building the world as it should be."

Michelle LaVaughn Robinson was born in Chicago on January 17, 1964. Her father, Fraser Robinson III, nicknamed her Miche. Fraser worked as a pump operator for the city of Chicago's water department. Her mother, Marian, stayed at home to raise Michelle and her brother Craig, who is sixteen months older. Later, she worked as a secretary.

Michelle grew up in a cozy—if not cramped—house on Chicago's South Side. The four-room bungalow belonged to an aunt who lived downstairs and rented the top floor to Michelle's family. The aunt, a piano teacher, taught Michelle

A 2008 photo of Michelle's mother, Marian *(Courtesy of AP Images/M. Spencer Green)*

to play, and Marian Robinson recalled that her daughter "would practice the piano for so long you'd have to tell her to stop."

Michelle didn't have a room of her own: a divider in the living room partitioned off what served as her bedroom. A childhood friend described Michelle's bedroom as "the smallest room I had ever seen. It was like a closet." Craig described the family's home to a reporter by saying: "If I had to describe it to a real estate agent, it would be one bedroom, one bathroom. If you said that it was eleven hundred square feet, I'd call you a liar."

Marian tutored her children, and both learned to read before they started school. From an early age Michelle proved to be strong-willed, independent, and competitive. Once, an elementary school teacher complained about Michelle's temper, but Marian Robinson told the teacher, "yeah, she's got a temper. But we decided to keep her anyway!"

When not practicing the piano, Michelle loved to play with her Easy-Bake Oven and Barbie dolls. TV was off limits, except for one hour a night. Instead, Fraser and Marian Robinson expected Michelle and Craig to spend their spare time reading books, playing sports, and engaging in dinnertime conversations. The siblings also had chores. "We alternated washing dishes," Craig recalled. "I had Monday, Wednesday, Friday. Michelle had Tuesday, Thursday, Saturday." It was also Michelle's job to scrub the sink, mop the floor, and clean the toilet.

When Fraser was thirty, he came down with multiple sclerosis, a debilitating disease. Still, he kept his job and continued to provide for his family. He compensated for his worsening health by getting up an hour earlier than usual to get ready for work. Eventually, Fraser needed two canes to walk and the simplest tasks became time consuming ordeals. Yet, he worked as long as he was physically able.

The Robinsons weren't regular churchgoers. Fraser and Marian raised their children with a sense of what was right and wrong, but they always encouraged them to think for themselves and to be unafraid of questioning authority.

"More important, even, than learning to read and write, was to teach them to think," Marian said. "We told them, 'Make sure you respect your teachers, but don't hesitate to question them. Don't even allow us to say anything to you. Ask us why."

Still, the Robinsons were able to show their authority to make sure their children behaved. Fraser would exert his authority in a quiet, but unquestioned way. If Michelle or Craig misbehaved, he could discipline them without even raising his voice. He would just give the misbehaving a child an icy stare and say: "I'm disappointed." Those two disapproving words were enough to make the children cry.

"You never wanted to disappoint him," Michelle recalled. "We would be bawling."

Fraser's limited income as a city worker kept the Robinsons at home most of the time. On weekends the family stayed in and played games like Monopoly or Chinese Checkers. Craig Robinson recalled that he and his sister also played a game they called "Office," in which Michelle showed early signs that she knew how to take command. "She was the secretary, and I was the boss. But she did everything. It was her game, and I kind of had nothing to do."

Sunday evenings the family visited Fraser's parents, Fraser Robinson Jr. and his wife LaVaughn, who lived nearby. During the summer, the family usually spent a week at a Michigan getaway called Duke's Happy Holiday Resort. And starting at about age ten, Michelle and her family began to make regular trips to Georgetown, South Carolina. Fraser Robinson Jr. had migrated to Chicago from Georgetown in the early 1930s. Like millions of other African Americans, he had journeyed north in hopes of a better life. After he retired though, he and his wife returned to Georgetown.

Michelle's parents hoped that she and Craig would one day enjoy and afford some of the material things that they couldn't provide. They believed that the key to improved economic opportunities was a good education.

"We had very hardworking parents," Michelle recalled. "They didn't go to college, but they believed in the importance of education; they were staunch supporters of us, so we always had two parents telling us how wonderful we were."

Michelle and Craig were both good students, and both skipped the second grade. Craig grew to become a six-foot, six-inch high-school basketball star. He was also a gifted student. His academic success and his athletic skills helped him to earn a scholarship to Princeton University.

Michelle was encouraged to emulate her brother, but she had no interest in high school sports. Craig remembered how that encouragement to be more like him backfired. "That's the best way not to get her to do something. She didn't want to play just because she was tall, black and athletic."

When she did play, Michelle demonstrated athletic skill and a strong competitive spirit. In neighborhood pick-up basketball games with Craig and his friends, she could easily compete with the boys. However, she decided to concentrate on academics instead of athletics.

Sibling rivalry with her gifted brother encouraged Michelle to work harder and do better. Mother Marian recalled: "She used to have a little bit of trouble with tests, so she did whatever she had to, to make up for that. I'm sure that it was psychological because she was hardworking and she had a

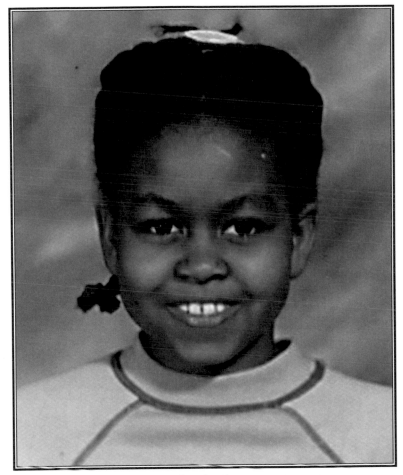

Michelle in grade school *(Courtesy of Polaris)*

brother who could pass a test just by carrying a book under his arm. When you are around someone like that, even if you are OK, you want to be as good or better."

In the sixth grade, Michelle was admitted into a program for gifted students at what is now Bouchet Elementary school. She graduated as class salutatorian.

She attended Whitney M. Young High School. There, she took advanced placement classes, served as the student council

Michelle's yearbook picture, taken when she was the student council treasurer. *(Courtesy of Whitney M. Young High School)*

treasurer, consistently made the honor roll, and became good friends with the daughter of the Rev. Jesse Jackson, Santita, who later would sing at the Obamas' wedding and become godmother to their first daughter.

After graduating from high school in 1981, Michelle decided, like Craig, to attend Princeton. Yet, even with good grades and a record of achievement, some of Michelle's teachers told her that her grades and test scores weren't good enough to get her admitted to an Ivy League school. Michelle knew better.

Michelle (center) poses with other students after being inducted in the National Honor Society. *(Courtesy of Whitney M. Young High School)*

Michelle (left) standing with other high school junior class officers. *(Courtesy of Whitney M. Young High School)*

Her feeling was that if her brother could get into Princeton, then she could too.

"A black kid from the South Side of Chicago that plays basketball and is smart. He was getting in everywhere," Michelle said about her brother. "But I knew him and I knew his study habits, and I was like, 'I can do that too.'" Michelle's beliefs proved correct: she was accepted into Princeton.

Michelle (back row, sixth from left) with other members of the executive board of the student council. *(Courtesy of Whitney M. Young High School)*

When Michelle entered Princeton in the fall of 1981, she found that she had bigger concerns than living in the shadow of her basketball star brother. At that time, blacks and other minority students were often not warmly received by their white classmates.

The mother of Michelle's first roommate complained to the faculty when she learned that her daughter, who is white, had to share a room with an African American. "I was horrified," the mother said. "I told them we weren't used to living with black people—[my daughter] is from the South."

In other instances, it may have been more resentment than racism. There was a prevailing attitude that affirmative-action programs had kept deserving white students out of Princeton, while letting less-qualified minority students get admitted.

In spite of these attitudes, or perhaps in retaliation against them, Michelle was unabashedly outspoken.

"Michelle's always been very vocal about anything," her mother recalled. "If it's not right she's going to say so. When she was at Princeton, her brother called me and said, 'Mom, Michelle's here telling people they're not teaching French right.' She thought that the style was not conversational enough. I told him, 'Just pretend that you don't know her.'"

Angela Acree, a former college roommate and close friend of Michelle, remembers Princeton as "a very sexist, segregated place." She also recalled how black and Hispanic students were asked to attend some special classes, a few weeks before the start of freshman year. University officials said that it was to help them make the transition to college, but Acree felt that she and the other minority students were already well prepared for the college life and environment.

Michelle followed her brother's footsteps and attended Princeton University in New Jersey. Shown here is Nassau Hall, the school's oldest building.

"We weren't sure whether they thought we needed an extra start or they just said, 'Let's bring all the black kids together.'"

Acree and Michelle spent a lot of time with Suzanne Alele, another black student who felt snubbed and sometimes isolated. They would talk about white classmates who would walk by them on campus and pretend not to see them. They would often meet at a social club called the Third World Center.

Michelle didn't let the way she was received by other students affect her studies. She graduated cum laude (with honors) in 1985. She majored in sociology, with a minor in

African American studies. She wrote a senior thesis entitled "Princeton Educated Blacks and the Black Community."

In the thesis, she wrote about how the university could have done more to aid and assist minority students:

"Unfortunately, there are very few adequate support groups which provide some form of guidance and counsel for Black students having difficulty making the transition from their home environments to Princeton's environment. Most students are dependent upon the use of their own faculties to carry them through Princeton."

In the introduction to the thesis, Michelle avoided using the word racism, but she made it clear that her race often made her feel more like than a visitor than a student.

> My experiences at Princeton have made me far more aware of my "Blackness" than ever before. I have found that at Princeton no matter how liberal and open-minded some of my White professors and classmates try to be toward me, I sometimes feel like a visitor on campus; as if I really don't belong. Regardless of the circumstances under which I interact with Whites at Princeton, it often seems as if, to them, I will always be a Black first and a student second.

Michelle's feelings of exclusion and perceptions of racism weren't something that she shared with her parents.

"She didn't talk about it a lot," Marian recalled. "I just learned from reading some articles that she did feel different from other people. But she never let that bother her."

After graduating from Princeton, Michelle quickly moved on to her next goal: law school. She applied to Harvard Law School, and once again, people told her that her grades and test scores weren't good enough to get her admitted to a prestigious Ivy League school. Once again, Michelle ignored the doubters and proved them wrong. She was admitted to Harvard Law in 1985.

At Harvard, Michelle was a successful student. Professor Randall Kennedy knew both Michelle and her future husband Barack when they attended Harvard Law School at different times. "When [Barack Obama] spoke, people got quiet and listened," Kennedy recalled. "Michelle had a quieter, lower profile." Still, Michelle participated in many political demonstrations, including some advocating the hiring of minority professors.

Michelle graduated from Harvard Law in 1988, with a Juris Doctor (doctor of law) degree. After graduation, she took a position with the Chicago law firm Sidley Austin. It was a large corporate firm, where she specialized in intellectual property and entertainment law. Early in her tenure with the firm, she was assigned to mentor a summer hire that had just completed his first year at Harvard Law School.

The summer hire was named Barack Obama. Soon he would begin to change Michelle's life in ways she never expected.

two
This Guy is Different

Before she met Barack Obama, Michelle Robinson heard some office talk about a handsome and smart summer hire she would be advising. However, she had her doubts:

> I was skeptical at first. Everyone was raving about this smart, attractive, young first-year associate they recruited from Harvard. Everyone was like, "Oh, he's brilliant, he's amazing and he's attractive." I said, "Okay, this is probably just a Brother who can talk straight." Then I heard that he grew up in Hawaii. Weird background, so I said he's probably a little odd, strange. I already had in my mind that this guy was going to be lame.

But after meeting the young law student, Michelle wondered if she had been too quick to judge Barack. "First, he was more attractive than his picture," she recalled. "He came in confident, at ease with himself. He was easy to talk to and had a good sense of humor."

They first met when they were introduced early one morning at the office. Later, Barack couldn't recall what he and Michelle talked about at their first meeting, but he remembered in detail how she looked and what she wore. "I remember that she was tall—almost my height in heels—and lovely, with a friendly professional manner that matched her tailored suit and blouse."

Later that day, they met again for lunch, and got to know each other further. Michelle learned that Barack had doubts about pursuing a career as a corporate lawyer. He was more interested in working in the public sector and later going into politics. But he had growing debts because of his student loans, and when Sidley Austin offered him three months of relatively lucrative employment, he wasn't in a position to turn it down. Barack learned all about Michelle's background, her family and her career plans. She made it clear that her career plans couldn't be sidetracked by distractions like men and romance.

Barack noticed that she seemed to be enjoying his company and that she wasn't in a hurry to get back to the office. And he was intrigued by her as well:

> She knew how to laugh, brightly and easily . . . And there was something else, a glimmer that danced across her round, dark eyes whenever I looked at her with the slightest hint of uncertainty, as if, deep inside, she knew how fragile things really were, and that is she ever let go, even for a moment, all her plans might quickly unravel. That touched me somehow, that trace of vulnerability. I wanted to know that part of her.

At that time, Michelle wasn't expecting a business lunch to lead to romance. Yet, she couldn't deny that maybe there was something to all that office talk that she had been hearing about that new summer hire. "We went out to lunch that first day and I was really impressed," she said.

Still, Michelle rebuffed Barack when he asked her out on a date. She told him that it was inappropriate because she was his summer advisor. Barack persisted, telling Michelle that just one date wouldn't be a serious violation of company policy. Once, he even joked about quitting so they would be free to date. Michelle was still hesitant, though.

Barack Obama at Harvard Law School in 1990, around the time he began dating Michelle. *(Courtesy of Steve Liss/Time Life Pictures/Getty Images)*

They did begin spending time together socially. He escorted her to some parties and saw her at some of the firm's outings and social events. Michelle even tried to fix him up with a couple of her friends. That didn't work. Barack wasn't interested in dating anyone else.

While they were spending time together as friends, Michelle accompanied Barack to a community organizing meeting in a church basement. Barack rose during the meeting, and delivered an inspiring speech about changing things from "the world as it is, and the world as it should be."

Michelle had already seen that Barack had looks, brains, manners, and wit. But now she was witnessing a new side of him, a seriousness that had been lacking in other men she had dated.

"I was like, 'This guy is different,'" she said. "He is really different, in addition to being nice and funny and cute and all that. He's got a seriousness and commitment that you don't see every day."

Still, before agreeing to go out on a date with Barack, Michelle asked her brother to play basketball with him. "Not to see [how good a] player he was," Craig recalled, "but because she'd grown up hearing my dad and I say you can tell a lot about a guy on the basketball court."

Craig said he found "no personality flaws with respect to the basketball evaluation," so about a month after Barack first asked Michelle out, she gave in. Their first real date was a visit to the gallery of the Chicago Art Institute, followed by seeing the movie *Do the Right Thing.* They continued dating throughout the summer.

Soon, Barack met Michelle's parents, and he compared her family to the perfect family that you would see on a TV show.

> It wasn't until I met Michelle's family that I began to understand her. It turned out that visiting the Robinson household was like dropping in on the set of *Leave It to Beaver.* There was Fraser, the kindly, good-humored father who never missed a day of work or any of his son's ball games. There was Marian, the pretty sensible mother who baked birthday cakes, kept order in the house, and had volunteered at school to make sure her children were behaving . . . There was Craig, the basketball star brother, tall and friendly and courteous and funny, working as an investment banker but dreaming of going into coaching someday.

Barack and Michelle visited the Chicago Art Institute on their first real date together. *(Courtesy of Sarah Hadley/Alamy)*

The Robinsons were the stable, two-parent family that Barack had missed out on when he was growing up (his parents had divorced when he was two, and he barely knew his father). He wrote that visiting Michelle's family "stirred a longing for stability and a sense of place that I had not realized was there."

Craig Robinson

Like his sister, Michelle, Craig Robinson is a Princeton graduate and a person of achievement and accomplishment. Since 2006, Michelle's big brother has been a head basketball coach, first at Brown University and then at Oregon State University in Corvallis, Oregon.

During his college basketball career, Robinson was twice honored as the Ivy League's Player of the Year. He also played in two NCAA Tournaments and led the Ivy League in field goal percentage in 1982 and 1983. He ranks fourth on Princeton's all-time scoring list with 1,441 points.

After graduating from Princeton in 1983 with a degree in sociology, Robinson was drafted by the Philadelphia 76ers in the fourth round of the 1983 NBA draft. He didn't play in the NBA, but he did play professional basketball for two years for the Manchester (England) Giants in the European Basketball League. During that time, he also served as the assistant to the general manager and as the team's public relations officer.

Robinson began his coaching career as an assistant coach at the Illinois Institute of Technology from 1988

Michelle's brother, Craig Robinson, coaching the Brown University men's basketball team in 2007. *(Courtesy of AP Images)*

to 1990. Then, he took a break from coaching to earn an MBA in finance from the University of Chicago. From 1990 to 1999, he worked as a bond trader for Continental Bank, Morgan Stanley, Dean Witter, and Loop Capital Markets.

In or around 2000, Robinson returned to coaching, becoming an assistant at Northwestern. He stayed there until 2006 before being hired by Brown University. Robinson's tenure at Brown was short, but successful. After his first season there, *Basketball U.*, a Web site covering Division 1 basketball, named him the Ivy League Men's Basketball Coach of the Year. In his second season, he led the Brown Bears to a 19-10 record and an 11-3 mark in Ivy League play. The nineteen wins set a school record for most wins in a season.

Robinson's success at Brown led to Oregon State pursuing and hiring him as their head basketball coach. Upon his hiring, Brown Athletic Director Michael Goldberger praised his performance, saying:

> I'm delighted for Craig, but having him leave Brown is a big loss for our university. Craig did a fabulous job at Brown. He was successful on the court, he connected with the student-athletes and was a role model for all students. Craig made this a better basketball program. While Craig's success has made our search to hire a top coach much easier, I wish we didn't lose him.

Fraser, Marian, and Craig were all favorably impressed with Barack, but they knew that Michelle could be a demanding girlfriend. She had a history of breaking up with other suitors. It was a family joke that sooner or later, Michelle would cast him aside. "The first thing I was worried about was, is this guy going to make the cut?" Craig said. "How long is it going to be till he gets fired?"

At the end of the summer, Barack and Michelle parted, as Barack had to return to law school in Boston. They continued to stay in touch, though, maintaining a long distance relationship. "Before I met Michelle, I was too immature to hold something like that together," Barack said.

While Michelle and Barack were separated, her father Fraser, who had been in poor health since his thirties, underwent a kidney operation. There were some unexpected complications, though, and Fraser died.

Six months after leaving Chicago, Barack returned to Chicago to attend Fraser's funeral. When he stood with Michelle at her father's gravesite, Barack was feeling a growing love that was understood, if not expressed. "I realized that in some unspoken, still tentative way, she and I were already becoming a family."

Still, Michelle and Barack didn't agree on whether marriage was a necessary step in starting a family. "We would have this running debate throughout our relationship about whether marriage was necessary," Michelle recalled. "It was sort of a bone of contention, because I was like, 'Look buddy, I'm not one of these who'll just hang out forever.' You know that's not who I am. He was like – 'Marriage, it doesn't mean anything, it's really how you feel.' And I was, like, 'Yeah right.'"

Barack eventually realized that Michelle was serious about matrimony. If he didn't marry her, there was a genuine chance of losing her. They went to dinner one night at Gordon's, a Chicago restaurant. Before desert, Barack started another discussion about whether marriage was still meaningful as a modern day institution. Michelle was angered, and responded by telling Barack that he needed to start getting serious about their relationship. It was a replay of a discussion that they'd had several times before. The discussion was briefly interrupted when the waiter arrived with their desert. There was a small box on the plate, and inside the box was an engagement ring from Barack.

Michelle recalled that he said: "Kind of shuts you up, doesn't it?" She tried on the ring, and accepted his proposal. "I don't think I even ate [desert]," Michelle said. "I was so shocked and sort of a little embarrassed because he did sort of shut me up."

After they were engaged, they traveled to Hawaii and Kenya so Michelle could meet Barack's extended family. They also began planning for their wedding.

Barack had graduated from Harvard Law School in 1991, and returned to Chicago to begin his career and be with Michelle. Michelle didn't see much of him though, as he spearheaded a voter registration drive for the 1992 presidential election.

The drive was called the Illinois Project Vote and it was credited with getting more than 150,000 new voters registered. Most of the new voters were low income African Americans living in or around Chicago. While he worked, Michelle continued her law career at Sidley Austin.

During this time, Barack and Michelle discussed his ambition to get involved in politics. Michelle encouraged him on: "I told him, 'If that's what you really want to do, I think that you would be great at it. You are everything that people say they want in public officials.'"

On October 18, 1992, Michelle Robinson and Barack Obama were married at the Trinity United Church of Christ in Chicago. The ceremony was performed by Rev. Jeremiah A. Wright, Jr., who would later become a controversial figure in the Obamas' lives.

Michelle and Barack were married on
October 18, 1992. *(Courtesy of AP Images)*

Since the 1992 presidential election was just two weeks away, they had a very brief honeymoon, as Barack was busy with his voter registration work. Politics was already affecting their marriage, and it would continue to do so.

three
Serving the Public

Michelle and Barack settled into a residence in the Hyde Park neighborhood on Chicago's South Side. The neighborhood had a history of being a place where large numbers of whites, blacks, and mixed-race couples lived together. It was also regarded as a trendy place for young, upwardly mobile blacks.

Despite their status as recent graduates of Harvard Law School, neither Michelle nor Barack were making a lot of money. After the death of her father and a former college roommate, Michelle had decided to leave corporate law and work in public service. Her time with Sidley Austin had been lucrative, but unfulfilling. Shortly before marrying Barack, Michelle left the firm.

"I started thinking about the fact that I went to some of the best schools in the country and that I have no idea of what I want to do," Michelle said. "That kind of stuff got me worked up because I thought, 'This isn't education. You can make money and have a nice degree. But what are you learning about giving back to the world, and finding your passion and letting that guide you as opposed to the school that you got into?'"

Seeking fulfillment, and hoping to improve her community, Michelle went to work for the city of Chicago. She served as an assistant to the mayor of Chicago, Richard M. Daley, and as assistant commissioner of planning and development. In 1993, she was named executive director for the Chicago office of Public Allies. The office of Public Allies was a nonprofit organization that encouraged young people to work on improving their communities through other nonprofit groups and government agencies.

However, leaving her high-paying job at Sidley Austin had been a considerable financial sacrifice for the young couple. Both Michelle and Barack had substantial student loans that had to be repaid. Michelle worried that the loans would never get paid off. But Barack convinced her that by living frugally, their combined incomes would eventually pay off the loans.

After the election of President Bill Clinton in 1992, Project Vote had disbanded and Barack found a new job that made up for Michelle's diminished salary. He joined the Chicago law firm of Miner, Barnhill & Galland. The firm suited Barack's desire to be a force for social change and good: it specialized in discrimination and civil rights cases. Barack also had started writing his autobiography. After working a full day, he'd come home and immerse himself in his writing. Michelle was understanding, but she couldn't avoid having some feelings of loneliness and neglect. She had a habit of going to bed early while Barack was still writing.

Having different sleeping schedules and money problems may have been the least of their problems as newlyweds. Michelle and Barack had come from two very different backgrounds. They had differing expectations and conceptions of what their marriage was going to be like. Michelle recalled:

> I came into our marriage with a more traditional notion of what a family is. It was what I knew growing up—the mother at home, the father works, you have dinner around the table. I had a very stable, conventional upbringing, and that felt very safe to me. And then I married a man who came from a very different kind of upbringing. He didn't grow up with a father; his mother traveled the world. So we both came to this marriage with very different notions about what children need, and what does a couple need to be happy.

Barack agreed that making their marriage work took a lot of work, and that the adjustments took years, not weeks or months.

"For the first few years of our marriage, Michelle and I went through the usual adjustments all couples go through: learning to read each other's moods, accepting the quirks and habits of a stranger underfoot," Barack said. "Michelle liked to wake up early and could barely keep her eyes open after ten o'clock. I was a night owl and could be a bit grumpy (mean, Michelle would say) within the first half hour or so of getting out of bed. . . . What I considered normal often left Michelle feeling lonely."

Barack admitted that his tendency to take on too much has been a recurring problem. He said, "There are times that

I want to do everything and be everything. . . . And that can sometimes get me into trouble. That's historically been one of my bigger faults. I mean, I was trying to organize Project Vote at the same time as I was writing a book and there are only so many hours in the day."

Barack eventually finished his autobiography, entitled *Dreams from My Father.* The book was first published in 1995, but it didn't sell well at that time. Years later, after Barack became a nationally known political figure, it made the best seller list. But at the time, the writing put an undeniable strain on Michelle and Barack's marriage.

Michelle spoke about what she saw as her husband's self-absorption, and a perceived difference between men and women. "What I notice about men, all men, is that there order is me, my family, God is in there somewhere, but 'me' is first. And for women, 'me' is fourth and that's not healthy."

Things were only going to get more complicated for the young couple. Barack's work with the voter registration project had whetted his political ambitions. In 1995, an opportunity to run for public office materialized. Barack quickly acted to seize the opportunity.

Alice Palmer was serving her first term in the Illinois State Senate, when she decided to run for Congress. Barack decided to run for the abandoned seat in the state senate, and she supported his bid to succeed her. According to Barack, she also said that she would retire from politics if she wasn't elected to Congress. But after losing the congressional primary election, Palmer decided she wanted to return to the seat in the state senate that she had vacated.

Palmer's supporters had asked Barack to drop out of the race and let her reclaim her former seat. Barack flatly

Barack's 2004 edition of his autobiography, *Dreams from My Father*.
(Courtesy of AP Images/Seth Perlman)

refused. He had too much time and money invested in his first run for office, and he felt that Palmer had gone back on her word.

Palmer filed to run for her old state senate seat. She had to file a nominating petition to get into the race. In about ten days, she got more than enough people to sign her petition. But one of Barack's supporters challenged the legality of the signatures.

A date was set for a hearing about the legality of the signatures on petitions submitted by Palmer and other candidates running against Barack. The major technicality was that many voters printed their names on the petitions when the law required them to sign their names. Palmer and her supporters gathered affidavits from the voters who printed their names, but they quickly realized that they wouldn't be able to correct the problem before the hearing.

Obama campaigning in 1995 for the Illinois State Senate.

Palmer dropped out of the race, and Barack's other opponents were disqualified by the elections board. He won the nomination and the election, running unopposed.

Michelle experienced some mixed emotions over her husband's election. She had long been aware of his passion for politics. She knew that it was inevitable that someday he would run for office—it just came sooner that she had expected. They had only been married for four years. When he had first approached her with the idea of running for the state senate, she had been strongly negative.

"I said, 'I married you because you're cute and your smart, but this is the dumbest thing you could have asked me to do,'" she told a reporter. "Fortunately for all of us, Barack wasn't as cynical as I was."

Barack's election to the state senate meant that they would be separated for days at a time when the legislature was in session. It was the start of what became a recurring pattern in their marriage. During the week, Barack would be away, working in the state senate. During the weekends, he would be back at home reconnecting with Michelle.

Michelle continued to work full time. In 1996, she had started a new job as the associate dean of Student Services at the University of Chicago, where she continued to work to improve her community by developing the university's Community Service Center. Her work was a source of great satisfaction, and before long the need for a second income became essential. In 1999, Michelle gave birth to a daughter, Malia Ann.

Though Michelle and Barack were thrilled by the birth of their daughter, finances remained tight for the couple. Reportedly, Michelle and Barack still owed more than

An undated photo of Barack lecturing at the University of Chicago's law school. *(Courtesy of AP Images)*

$100,000 in student loans. Barack took a second job as a lecturer at the University of Chicago's law school, and he continued to practice law part time. This helped the Obamas financially, but served to lessen the already small amount of time they had together.

The Obamas' finances and the amount of time Barack had for his family were further strained when Barack decided that he would run for Congress in 2000. After only four years in the state senate, he wanted to hold an office that offered more power, prestige, and opportunity for advancement. Michelle, however, wasn't enthused about her husband running for Congress.

"Michelle put up no pretense of being happy with the decision," Barack recalled. "My failure to clean up the kitchen suddenly became less endearing. Leaning down to kiss Michelle good-bye in the morning, all I would get was a peck on the cheek. . . . 'You only think about yourself,' she would tell me. 'I never thought I'd have to raise a family alone.'"

Michelle's words stung Barack, but they served as a wake-up call. He suddenly realized how one-sided their relationship had become. "No matter how much I told myself that Michelle and I were equal partners, and that her dreams and ambitions were my own—the fact was that when children showed up, it was Michelle and not I who was expected to make the necessary adjustments. Sure I helped out, but it was always on my terms, on my schedule," Barack said.

He began making a concerted effort to spend more time with his family, but this would come back to hurt him during his run for Congress.

In December 1999, Michelle, Barack, and Malia took their annual family vacation to Hawaii. The yearly getaway offered a romantic reconnect for the young couple and a welcome break from politics. But in 1999, the Illinois General Assembly was having a heated debate over a gun control bill.

Normally, the General Assembly wouldn't be in session between Christmas and New Year's Day. But a special session had been called. Barack had already shortened his family vacation from two weeks to five days. Michelle had got-

Michelle with daughters Malia (center) and Natasha (left) at Disney World in 2007. *(Courtesy of AP Images)*

ten tired of tolerating her husband's frequent absences to advance his political career, and Malia had come down with a bad cold during the abbreviated vacation.

When the gun control measure came up for a vote, Barack was still vacationing in Hawaii. It fell three votes short of passing and Barack was one of the three state senators that Illinois governor George Ryan had counted on to vote for the measure. Without mentioning Barack by name, Governor Ryan expressed his great disappointment by saying: "I'm angered, frankly, that the senate didn't do a better job."

Barack's decision to stay on vacation may have been right for his family, but many were quick to use it against him. His opponent in the upcoming 2000 congressional race, incumbent congressman Bobby Rush, hammered away at Barack's

Bobby Rush (center) celebrates his primary victory over Barack in 2000. *(Courtesy of AP Images)*

Barack stands with Michelle and Malia as he gives his concession speech after losing his 2000 bid for Congress. *(Courtesy of AP Images/Frank Polich)*

absence during a crucial vote. Rush also attacked Barack as an excessively ambitious young upstart unworthy of replacing an experienced Washington insider.

Rush's attacks resonated with the voters and Barack was beaten in the primary election, by a two-to-one margin. There was little time to dwell on his defeat though. In 2001, Michelle gave birth to her and Barack's second daughter, Natasha.

four
Mounting Pressures

With Barack spending much of his time of the past several years campaigning for his failed congressional bid, Michelle had been left with doing most of the parenting and the housekeeping duties. With the birth of their second daughter, Natasha (called Sasha) in 2001, Barack promised he'd be a more committed husband and father. But things had already become strained and difficult for the couple, especially in regards to their finances.

Barack had spent over half a million dollars on his Congressional campaign. Michelle and Barack's combined income was more than $250,000 a year, but the losing congressional campaign had put them even deeper in debt. They were still repaying their student loans and their credit cards were maxed out. Further, because both Michelle and Barack were working full time, they were paying for a caregiver to help care for their children.

Both Michelle and Barack were deeply concerned about their financial future. A low point occurred in the summer of 2000. Barack had flown to Los Angeles for the Democratic National Convention, and when he tried to rent a car at the airport, his credit card was rejected.

"I was broke," Barack recalled. "And not only that, but my wife was mad at me because we had a baby and I had made this run for Congress. . . . It wasn't a high point in my life."

Barack began paying more attention to money matters. He considered a career change such as working for a non-profit agency, or seeking full-time employment with the University of Chicago. That would have kept him closer to home and it would have made things easier for Michelle and their children.

Less than a year after his unsuccessful bid for Congress, Barack was approached by some party leaders about running for the office of Illinois attorney general. He rejected the idea by citing concerns about Michelle and the children.

"I put Michelle and the family through such heck with the congressional race and it put such significant strains on our marriage that I could not just turn around and start running all over again, so I passed that by."

While Barack's career had hit its first serious hurdle, and seemed to be in something of a standstill, Michelle's career was thriving. In 2002, Michelle interviewed for a job with University of Chicago Hospitals. Busy with her new baby Natasha, Michelle had to bring her daughter to the interview in a car-seat carrier. Still, she immediately impressed University of Chicago Hospitals' president, Michael Riordan, and he offered her a job as the hospital's executive director of community affairs.

Michelle proved incredibly effective in her new position. Over the next several years, she expanded the community affairs office from a staff of two to a staff of seventeen, and increased the number of volunteers to the hospital from two hundred to nearly one thousand.

Meanwhile, Barack's commitment to politics increased after the Democrats gained control of the Illinois State Senate in 2002. Becoming a member of the majority party gave him more power, prestige, and greater name recognition. Once again, Barack began thinking about running for a higher office. The only question was which one.

In 2004, the incumbent Republican U.S. senator from Illinois, Peter Fitzgerald, would be up for reelection. It's an axiom of politics that in a senate race the incumbent will have a decided advantage in name recognition, fund raising, and party support. Yet, Fitzgerald looked to be vulnerable because he had alienated himself from party leaders in Washington and Illinois. He had a reputation for being outspoken and unafraid of taking unpopular stands. Barack began to believe that he might be able to defeat Fitzgerald and win his seat in the U.S. Senate. But first he had to convince Michelle.

Michelle was against the idea of her husband running for the Senate for many valid reasons. Most of them were financial. They had two children, a mortgage, a maxed out credit card, and crushing student loan debt. Even if Barack somehow got elected to the Senate, it wouldn't help them financially.

"The big issue around the Senate for me was, how on earth can we afford it?" Michelle told an interviewer. "How are we going to get by? Okay, now we're going to have two households to fund, one here and one in Washington. We have law school debt, tuition to pay for the children, and we're trying to save for college for the girls . . . My thing was, this is ridiculous, even if you do win, how are you going to afford this wonderful next step in your life?"

Barack had a ready answer to her money worries—he would write another book. To Michelle, that idea sounded even crazier than unseating an incumbent senator. Barack's first book, *Dreams from My Father*, had only modest sales, despite generally favorable reviews. It seemed unlikely that writing another book would be their financial salvation.

So Barack tried another tactic. He told Michelle that if he didn't win the election, he'd get out of politics.

"What I told Michelle was that politics has been a huge strain on you, but I really think that there is a strong possibility that I can win this race. . . . I said to her that if you are willing to go with me on this ride and if it doesn't work out then I will step out of politics. . . . I think that she had come to realize that I would leave politics if she asked me to."

Barack's pledge broke down Michelle's resistance. From the day she first met him at Sidley Austin she had seen that he was a man with huge ambitions. At times, those ambitions may have sounded impractical to her, but she wasn't going to keep him from chasing his dream. She was even able to joke about the possibility of losing the election.

"Ultimately I capitulated and said, 'Whatever. We'll figure it out. We're not hurting. Go ahead,'" she said. Then she added, "'And maybe you'll lose.'"

Up until Barack's run for the Senate, Michelle had taken a mostly passive role in his political campaigns. She would show up at events where her presence was required, but that was generally the extent of her involvement. This time, though, she plunged into the campaign, starting with the fund-raising.

In the summer of 2002, Michelle accompanied Barack to a meeting with one of Chicago's wealthiest couples. Penny Pritzker's family had a fortune estimated to be in the billions. She and her husband, Bryan Traubert, had supported other Democrats and they were acquainted with Michelle and Barack.

During a lengthy jog, Penny and Bryan engaged the Obamas in a lengthy chat that covered everything from political views to philosophy of life. By the end of their jog, the wealthy couple had decided to support Barack.

"We had known Barack and Michelle previously, but we hadn't made up our minds about supporting him for the

A photo of Penny Sue Pritzker in 1989. Pritzker, whose family had a fortune estimated to be in the billions, helped to provide financial backing for Barack's 2004 Senate campaign. *(Courtesy of Getty Images)*

Senate," Pritzker recalled. "So Bryan and I had a long discussion about Barack and his values and the way that he carries himself, his family and the kind of human beings that he and Michelle are—what kind of people they are, as much as about lofty political ideals. . . . That was the seminal moment when we simply decided after that weekend that we would support them."

Once Penny began to back Barack, it became much easier for him to raise campaign funds. Still, he entered a crowded field of candidates. Eventually, six contenders entered the race for the Democratic nomination.

Illinois state comptroller Dan Hynes and multimillionaire businessman Blair Hull were a couple of the early favorites. In the initial stages of the race both of them ran ahead of Barack. Hynes enjoyed the support of both the Illinois House Speaker and Michael Madigan, the chairman of the state Democratic Party, and had the backing of most of Chicago's aldermen and the major labor unions.

Hull had the advantage of his family fortune. It's estimated that he spent $29 million of his own money on his campaign. By comparison, Barack's campaign raised and spent around $6 million. As the primary neared, Hull had a ten-point lead over Barack in the polls and Hynes was in third place.

Hull's campaign collapsed, though, after the *Chicago Tribune* reported that his ex-wife had taken out an order of protection against him in 1998. At first, Hull refused to discuss the matter by saying that it was irrelevant to his ability to be an effective senator. But pressure from the media got Hull and his ex-wife to make previously sealed divorce records public records. The records reported that Hull had been verbally abusive to his ex-wife.

Those revelations enabled Barack to surge into the lead. A week before the primary a *Chicago Tribune* poll showed him leading with 33 percent of the voters polled. Hynes had 19 percent and Hull had fallen to 16 percent. Hull and Hynes began intensifying their attacks on Barack, but his lead held up. In March 2004, Barack won the Democratic nomination with 53 percent of the vote.

In the general election, Barack faced another wealthy businessman in Republican challenger, Jack Ryan. Ryan attacked Barack as being too liberal for Illinois voters. However, for the second time, an unsealed divorce file torpedoed one of Barack's opponents.

Ryan had been married to Jeri Ryan, a television actress. They had divorced in 1999, and their divorce records had been sealed. However, rumors that Ryan had something to hide led to the *Chicago Tribune* and a Chicago television station suing to get the records unsealed. On June 21, 2004, a California judge unsealed the Ryan's divorce records.

What they revealed quickly and effectively ended Ryan's campaign and political future. The records showed that Ryan had taken his wife to sex clubs in three different cities and tried to force her into performing sexual acts in front of strangers. At first, Ryan denied most of the allegations. Then he tried arguing that his alleged behavior wasn't illegal.

While Ryan's campaign was crumbling, Barack avoided commenting on the charges by saying that it would be inappropriate. He was undoubtedly grateful that he and Michelle, despite their disagreements, enjoyed a strong and stable marriage.

Four days after the scandal broke, Ryan withdrew from the race. With the election about four-and-a-half months away,

Michelle speaking to students while on the campaign trail for Barack's 2004 run for Senate. *(Courtesy of AP Images/Jeff Roberson)*

the Republicans were without a candidate. For the next few weeks Barack enjoyed the luxury of campaigning without an opponent. Michelle continued to campaign for Barack and act as if nothing much had changed.

In one interview she emphasized that no one was taking Barack's election for granted. "Over the last few days, some people have said this is a done deal," she told reporter Krista Lewin. "But no one in our house has said that it is a done deal."

But even without an opponent in the Senate race, Michelle and Barack were unable to take any kind of break from politics. Things got even more hectic after Barack was chosen to deliver the keynote address at the 2004 Democratic National Convention. The success or failure of that speech could make or break Barack as a national political figure.

The Democratic National Committee had issued media credentials to 15,000 journalists, photographers, and commentators. The all-important keynote address would be heard and watched by millions of people all over the world. The 5,000 delegates would be the largest crowd that Barack had ever addressed. But before he delivered it, he rehearsed it in front of Michelle.

Michelle had always been his toughest critic and Barack knew that she could be brutally blunt. "We brought her into the practice room," Barack told some reporters. "Her assessment was that I wasn't going to embarrass the Obama family."

As the time neared for Barack to deliver the keynote address, Michelle saw that her usually poised and unflappable husband was getting nervous. She waited until just before Barack strode to the stage to calm him down. She did it with some gentle, affectionate teasing. "To break the tension, right before he went out on stage I leaned in close and said, 'Just don't screw it up, buddy.' We laughed and then Barack brought the house down."

Barack's keynote address became a defining moment in his political career. Even some partisan Republicans agreed that it had been an electrifying and inspiring address. Former Republican vice presidential candidate, Jack Kemp, called it a "fabulous speech." One prominent member of the Illinois Republican State Committee ruefully said, "I just wish that he was a Republican."

Michelle and Barack wave to the crowd after Barack's keynote address at the 2004 Democratic National Convention. *(Courtesy of AP Images)*

In early August 2004, the Illinois Republican State Central Committee met to pick a new senatorial candidate to oppose Barack. By that time Barack's keynote address had begun to make him a nationally known political figure. Picking an opponent had become a dispiriting task, but they couldn't let him run unopposed.

The Republican Party leaders picked Alan Keyes to replace Ryan. Keyes had never lived in Illinois or been elected to any political office. He was a Maryland resident, best known for

Barack debating with Alan Keyes (right), his Republican opponent in the 2004 Senate race. *(Courtesy of AP Images/Nam Y. Huh)*

being a former talk show host and a staunchly conservative African American. He had a history of making inflammatory remarks and he made a lot of them while running against Barack.

Keyes repeatedly attacked Barack, particularly his prochoice votes and views. At one news conference, he said that Jesus Christ wouldn't vote for Barack because of his votes against anti-abortion legislation.

Barack largely ignored Keyes' over-the-top rhetoric, and tried to use the campaign trail as a place for reconnecting with Michelle and his daughters. An RV was rented so the family of four could travel in the same vehicle, and they

Michelle stands with Barack and their daughters as she and Barack cast their votes in the 2004 Senate election. *(Courtesy of AP Images/Nam Y. Huh)*

were able to spend more time together. Still, Barack had little time for Michelle or his daughters: he was making up to eight speeches a day and was usually too preoccupied with campaigning to be spending much time being an attentive husband and father. It was extremely difficult to balance being a candidate with being a devoted family man.

"This was supposed to be a leisurely trip in an RV with my family. Instead it's turned into the Bataan Death March," Barack said ruefully. "So it's this delicate balance that I am still trying to figure out. . . . But we've got a campaign to run and we've got to get back to reality."

As Barack focused on his campaign, Michelle grew increasingly concerned for her husband's safety. As his campaign was gaining momentum, Barack was being increasingly mobbed by his supporters. She spoke to campaign staffers about hiring more security personnel, but they didn't want to put up a barrier between the candidate and the voters.

"I understand you have to achieve a balance between looking out for his safety and not looking like he is afraid of the community he is serving. But we have to find that balance," she said.

Michelle was deeply stressed by the long drives between campaign stops and the frequent demands on Barack's time. Through it all she gamely played the role of the politician's wife, always smiling for the cameras and standing by his side for photo ops.

On November 2, 2004, the long grueling, campaign finally ended. Barack was elected with a landslide total of 70 percent of the vote. He had reached his ambitious goal

Barack celebrates with Michelle and their daughters amid falling confetti after winning the 2004 Senate election. *(Courtesy of AP Images)*

of being elected to the U.S. Senate, and he had done it in a remarkably short time. Michelle had long known that Barack was a man of immense ambition. If she didn't already know, then she would soon learn exactly how immense that ambition was.

five
Balancing Family and Politics

*I*n January 2005, Barack took the oath of office as a U.S. senator with Michelle, Malia, and Natasha proudly looking on. While the family was walking out of the Capitol, six-year-old Malia innocently asked her father something that even Michelle couldn't ask publicly: "Daddy are you going to be president?"

Since there were several journalists nearby who heard the question, Barack didn't answer her. But even while he was running against Alan Keyes, he had worked at forming alliances with Democratic politicians outside of Illinois. During his senate campaign he traveled to Wisconsin, South Carolina, Colorado, and other states to campaign for other candidates.

Michelle's trip to Washington for Barack's swearing in was one of the few occasions she traveled to the capital. Barack

Barack stands with Michelle, their daughters, and Vice President Dick
Cheney as he's sworn in as a U.S. Senator in 2005. *(Courtesy of Alex Wong/*
Getty Images)

had wanted to move his family to Washington, but Michelle wanted to remain in Chicago.

There were many reasons for this. She and her daughters had no friends or family in Washington, but her mother and many of her closest friends were still in Chicago. Moving to Washington would have cost Michelle her job at the University of Chicago Hospitals, where she continued to thrive.

Barack had to be talked into the idea of living apart from his family. Once Michelle convinced him that it was the best course of action, he rented an apartment in Washington, and commuted back to Chicago every possible weekend.

Maintaining two residences had become financially feasible for the formerly cash-strapped Obamas. In December 2004, Barack received a $1.9 million advance for agreeing to write three books for Random House Publishers. Prior to that, his first book, *Dreams From My Father*, had been reissued in paperback, and following his successful speech at the Democratic National Convention, had sold around 350,000 copies.

With the sudden influx of cash, they were able to pay off all their debts, and invest for their children's future college education.

While Barack's lucrative book deal was a financial windfall, Michelle was also bringing in a significant income. In May 2005, she was promoted to vice president of community and external affairs for the University of Chicago Hospitals. The promotion boosted her salary considerably.

Michelle also took a position on the board of directors of a company called Treehouse Foods, a supplier that earned much of its income selling to Wal-Mart. Though this position aided the Obamas' income, it would be used against Michelle and her husband in the years to come.

In the meantime though, the greatly increased income allowed the Obamas to move from their cozy condo to a much more roomy $1.65 million mansion in Hyde Park, a prestigious Chicago neighborhood.

In Washington, though Barack was just a freshman senator, his steadily increasing political profile and broad appeal was fueling talk about a run for the presidency in 2008. When asked about his political future, Michelle insisted that putting his family first was still the top priority.

Michelle and Barack's Hyde Park home in Chicago *(Courtesy of Peter Barreras/ZUMA Press)*

"Our future is making sure Barack can get to our daughter's ballet recitals and balancing the demands of this current set of responsibilities with our need to build a strong family, and that's taking a lot of energy out of us now," she told *Ebony* magazine. "It's very difficult to think about something as massive as running for president at this time. That's not part of our day-to-day conversation."

With Barack busy in Washington, Michelle led a disciplined and structured life. Her days began at 4:30 in the morning with a workout on the treadmill. She then spent some time with her daughters and got them to school, then proceeded to her job at the University of Chicago Hospital. Though she hired a full-time housekeeper to help, Michelle still kept a hectic and busy schedule. "I still go to Target," she told one reporter. "I do my own shopping. I'm on the soccer field. I am, you know, struggling with work and a career."

For his part, and to maintain his connection to his family, Barack was usually able to make it home to Chicago every weekend. Generally, he'd stay with Michelle and his daughters from Thursday to Sunday. While it wasn't an ideal situation, Michelle claimed that was an improvement over when he was running for the Senate: "People ask how I'm handling his being away, and I say that he's home more now then when he was running [for office]. He's breaking his neck to get home on the weekends." Sundays in particular were devoted to family activities.

But Barack had become such a high-profile politician that private moments were becoming rarer. They were still able to take their annual family vacation to Hawaii over Christmas, and in August 2006, the family took another trip to Kenya to see Barack's family in Kenya. However, that trip was more like a never-ending media event than a relaxing family vacation. An entourage of reporters, photographers, and film crews dogged the Obamas and chronicled their every move.

In 1995, Michelle had been able to enjoy some genuinely private moments with Barack during their vacation to Kenya. In 2006, though, things were different. A two-day family safari in the Masai Mara, for example, was supposed to be a private event, but it became impossible to keep the media away.

"Barack and I joked the whole way that we have an armed escort now, and when we went in before, we just walked around from shop to shop," she recalled, comparing the current trip to the first time she visited Kenya with Barack. "To have it elevated like this was kind of surreal . . . There is a part of you that is embarrassed by the scene of it. Part of you wants to say, 'Can we tame this down a little bit? Does it have to be all this? This is out of hand.' That is my instinct and I know that is his instinct too—do we really need all this?"

Still, the visit was a good one for the Obama family. They were able to visit Barack's step-grandmother and an uncle, and they participated in a tree planting ceremony in Nairobi. They also put their fame and media attention to good use, trying to help the local population. One of the major media events of the trip occurred when Michelle and Barack publicly took an AIDS test at an American run mobile clinic in Kisumu, Kenya.

Around that time, around 1.2 million of Kenya's 32 million people were HIV positive. In the Kitsumu area where Barack's father had once lived, nearly 20 percent of the people were infected with the AIDS virus. One reason that the numbers were so high was because there was a strong social

Michelle taking a public AIDS test at a mobile clinic in Kenya. *(Courtesy of AP Images/Sayyid Azim)*

stigma against being tested for the virus. By taking the test themselves, Michelle and Barack showed that there was no shame in being tested.

"I and my wife are personally taking HIV tests," Barack told the thousands of spectators who had gathered outside the clinic. "And if someone all the way from America can come and do that, then you have no excuse."

Shortly after they returned from Kenya, Barack was due back on the campaign trail. Though he wasn't up for reelection until 2010, Barack was needed to campaign and raise funds for other Democratic candidates in the 2006 midterm elections. Party leaders had been very optimistic about the Democrats picking up seats in both the House and Senate.

Their optimism was well founded. A slumping economy, the lingering war in Iraq and the low approval ratings of President George W. Bush were plaguing the Republicans. Voters had become more receptive to the idea that a change was needed. Most political pundits were predicting gains for the Democrats, but the final results exceeded even the most hopeful expectations of the Democratic Party leaders.

The Democrats picked up five seats in the Senate and thirty-one in the House. After twelve years of Republican rule, both houses of Congress would be controlled by the Democrats. The Republicans were unable to take away a single Congressional or gubernatorial seat that was held by a Democrat.

For Barack, the Democratic sweep meant much more than just becoming a member of the majority party in the Senate. The presidency was looking more and more like an achievable goal. But before he could run, he had to get Michelle's approval.

The day after the midterm elections Barack met with his key advisors. They discussed Barack's possible candidacy for the 2008 Democratic presidential nomination. How to get Michelle's approval for Barack to run was a central part of their discussion.

They decided that the best strategy was to include Michelle in the discussions instead of making decisions without her.

That way, Michelle would know that her opinions were important and that her support was essential. In December 2006, Michelle gave her approval. Reportedly, the only condition she made was for Barack to quit smoking.

Michelle's approval wasn't surprising to her longtime friends. She had always been supportive of Barack's political ambitions, but his rapid ascendancy had forced her to make many difficult choices sooner than she expected.

"If Barack really wants this, Michelle will support him and do what's necessary," said Cassandra Butts, a friend of Michelle's from Harvard Law School. "That's always been their relationship."

In January 2007, Barack used his Web site to announce that he was forming an exploratory committee to determine if a run for the presidency was feasible. Then, on February 10, 2007, Barack formally announced his candidacy. The time and place were chosen for maximum effect and media coverage: he stood outside of the Old State Capitol Building in Springfield, Illinois, where Abraham Lincoln had once given a speech denouncing slavery and calling for the country to unite. Barack and Michelle held hands as they walked down a long catwalk leading to a wooden podium.

Braving a bone-chilling temperature of five degrees Fahrenheit, they waved to a cheering crowd of around 16,000 supporters, spectators, and members of the media.

Michelle stood back behind Barack while the crowd chanted "O-ba-ma! O-ba-ma!" Then, Barack walked up to podium, surveyed the crowd and began invoking what would become the main theme of his campaign: "I know that I haven't spent a lot of time learning the ways of Washington.

But I've been there long enough to know that the ways of Washington must change."

The notion of "change" was suddenly central to Michelle as well. From that day on, her every word, gesture, and emotion would be recorded and noted by the ever-present, unblinking eye of the media. She would come under attack for her statements and actions, and many moments from her past would get dragged into the spotlight. Whether she was ready or not, Michelle Obama was entering the world of presidential politics.

six

On the Campaign Trail

Before the 2008 presidential race, Michelle had always been quietly supportive of Barack's political career. But it had always been more of a passive support than an active advocacy. "I've never participated at this level in any of his campaigns," she admitted. "I have usually chosen to just appear when necessary."

In Barack's other campaigns, Michelle had largely been spared from attacks and scrutiny. But as she took a very active role in his presidential campaign, she was considered fair game. An editorial in *USA Today* explained how the role and the public perception of a presidential candidate's wife had markedly changed since the 1950s:

> Since then, the role of most spouses has grown larger. And the more involved that they are in the campaigns, the more legitimate they are as a topic of debate. Like it or not, spouses

have become an important part of the process. They do not deserve to be dragged into the mud. But, nor are they entitled to blanket immunity.

In previous presidential elections, there have been other attacks on the wives of the candidates. When Michael Dukakis was the Democratic nominee in 1998, his wife, Kitty, came under attack. Senator Steven Symms of Idaho claimed that there were photographs of her burning a flag at an antiwar rally. Michael Dukakis denied the charges and no one was able to produce any such photos.

During the 2004 presidential election Teresa Heinz Kerry, the wife of Democratic nominee John Kerry was accused of using the term "un-American" in a speech. Some conservative Web sites also accused her of having links to terrorists; neither charge was ever proven.

Attacks on Michelle Obama started shortly after Barack began campaigning. One of the earliest attacks on Michelle was a credible one that she couldn't deny. In May 2007, political pressures led to her resigning her membership from the board of TreeHouse Foods. TreeHouse Foods was a major supplier to the corporate retail giant, Wal-Mart. Since Barack had criticized Wal-Mart for its labor practices, it looked very hypocritical for his wife to working for a company so closely affiliated with them. Fortunately, Michelle's quick resignation prevented a perceived conflict of interest from becoming a lingering political issue.

In her resignation statement, Michelle avoided mentioning any conflict with her husband's views and statements. She merely said that the rigors of the presidential campaign were keeping her from focusing on her work with TreeHouse

Foods. "As my campaign commitments continue to ramp up, it is becoming more difficult for me to provide the type of focus that I would like on my professional responsibilities. My priorities, particularly at this important time, are ensuring that our young daughters feel a sense of comfort and normalcy in this process, and that I can support my husband in his presidential campaign to bring much needed change."

The same month she severed ties with TreeHouse Foods, Michelle cut back on her hours at the University of Chicago Hospitals. She reduced them from forty to eight hours a week and took a proportionate 80 percent cut in pay. This freed her up to spend more time campaigning for Barack.

With Michelle out of TreeHouse, Barack's political enemies sought out new ways to target him and his wife. Thus far the largest sustained attack against Michelle had stemmed from a statement she made in Milwaukee, Wisconsin, in February 2008. While campaigning for Barack she said: "People in this country are ready for change, and hungry for a different kind of politics and . . . and for the first time in my adult lifetime, I am really proud of my country, and not just because Barack has done well, but because I think people are hungry for change."

Quickly, many conservative commentators took Michelle's statement out of context, reporting only part of the statement: "For the first time in my adult life, I am really proud of my country." Their attacks portrayed Michelle as being unpatriotic and unappreciative of her country. Cindy McCain, the wife of Barack's Republican opponent, John McCain, criticized Michelle by saying: "I don't know about you, if you heard those words earlier. I am very proud of my country."

But not all Republicans opted to attack Michelle for the controversial statement. She got an unexpected defense from the First Lady Laura Bush: "I think that she probably meant 'I'm more proud,' you know, is what she really meant. You have to be very careful in what you say. Everything that you say is looked at and in many cases misconstrued."

Michelle clarified her remark, explaining that she was proud of the political process for the first time. The large number of people that were becoming politically active and involved in the 2008 presidential election had made her proud of her country.

"I've had to clarify points that were misconstrued," she said. "But they're usually the same couple of points . . . I'm no different from Hillary (Rodham Clinton) or anyone else who has been a political target. There is a strategy involved. It's not personal."

Barack came to her defense by echoing her remarks: "What she meant was, this is the first time that she's been proud of politics in America," he said. "Because she's pretty cynical about the political process, and with good reason, and she's not alone. But she has seen large numbers of people get involved in the process, and she's encouraged."

Yet, no matter how may times the Obama campaign has explained the remark, it continues to be used. In May 2008, the Tennessee Republican Party used a video of Michelle's out-of-context remark in one of their attack ads. The ad showed various Tennessee residents giving different reasons why they were proud of America while it kept repeating Michelle's words. Both of Tennessee's Republican U.S. senators condemned the ad.

More attacks on Michelle were to follow. Some bloggers and conservative radio host Rush Limbaugh claimed that Michelle used the racial slur "whitey" while speaking from the pulpit of the Trinity United Church of Christ. The story was also reported on the conservative skewing Fox News Channel. Although the attackers claim that a video of the alleged incident exists, no one has been able to produce one.

Michelle addressed the "whitey" charge by making a reference to the 1970s sitcom *The Jeffersons*, in which the character George Jefferson was noted for making blustery racial remarks.

"You are amazed sometimes at how deep the lies can be," Michelle told one interviewer. "I mean, 'whitey?' That's something that George Jefferson would say. Anyone who says that doesn't know me. They don't know the life that I've lived. They don't know anything about me."

The repeated attacks on Michelle goaded Barack into challenging the media to come up with some proof. "If somebody has evidence that myself or Michelle or anybody has said something inappropriate, let them do it."

Failing to find any recent proof, the Obamas' opponents dug into Michelle's past for anything they could use against her. They began pressuring the Obamas and Princeton University to release Michelle's Princeton thesis, about the experience of black students at Princeton. Eventually, it was released to the media and the public.

In one section of the work, Michelle wrote about the attitudes of black Princeton alumni who attended the university in the 1970s: "It is possible that Black individuals either chose to or felt pressured to come together with other Blacks on campus because of the belief that Blacks must join in solidarity to combat a white oppressor. As the few Blacks in a White environment it is understandable that respondents might have felt a need to look out for one another."

Conservative commentators and bloggers, particulary Sean Hannity of Fox News's *Hannity and Colmes* took the words drastically out of context, omitting most of the text and reporting that Michelle Obama was a racist revolutionary who had written that "Blacks must join in solidarity to combat a white oppressor." Other news outlets, though, were quick to point out that Michelle's work was not advocating any racism or violence, but was documenting the racial issues at the relatively conservative environment of Princeton University in the 1970s and early 1980s.

To defend against the increasing number of erroneous reports and slurs about Barack and Michelle, Barack and his campaign aides launched an Internet counteroffensive. They launched a Web site called fightthesmears.com, intended to refute rumors and try to track their source. Along with dispelling rumors about Michelle (such as the "whitey" charge), the Web site refutes rumors that Barack was born in Kenya and that he was sworn in as a U.S. senator with his hand on a copy of the Koran.

Answering charges, explaining her words, and fending off attacks weren't the only things that were making things difficult for Michelle. After a few primaries, the once crowded field of Democratic candidates had been reduced to just two contenders: Barack and Senator Hillary Clinton. Michelle was placed in the difficult position of asking women voters to deny Clinton the opportunity to become America's first woman president.

Michelle talks with Hillary Clinton at a Democratic Party event in
2007. *(Courtesy of AP Images/Charlie Neibergall)*

Susan Carroll, a senior scholar at the Center for American Women and Politics, explained Michelle's dilemma, saying: "It puts the woman in the position of trying to argue . . . that her husband is better for women than a woman is for women. That's a very difficult argument to try and make, particularly if you've got a woman like Hillary Clinton who certainly doesn't shy away from feminism and hasn't shied away from the causes of women, children, and families."

When talking about Clinton, Michelle would praise her at

Michelle hugs Barack in front of an audience at a New Hampshire campaign rally. *(Courtesy of AP Images)*

times, but at other times, she went into the attack mode. She would say that Clinton had been a role model for how to be a First Lady. However, that didn't mean that she would be a better nominee than Barack. When she went on the attack, Michelle would say that Clinton represented "the same old thing over and over again."

Throughout the grueling primary campaign, neither Barack nor Clinton was able to quickly clinch the nomination. February 5, 2008 was called "Super Tuesday" because twenty-three primaries were held that day. It was hoped that a clear cut winner would emerge by winning most of those primaries. Barack won fourteen primaries, but Clinton kept the delegate vote close by winning primaries in the heavily populated states of California and New York.

Michelle and Barack's hopes of winning the nomination were buoyed later that month when Barack won ten straight primaries and caucuses; still, that left him several hundred delegates shy of cinching the nomination. Then, in the first week of March, Clinton came back by winning primaries in Ohio and Texas.

Both candidates continued to battle it out until June 7, 2008. On that date, Clinton announced that she was suspending her campaign and endorsing Barack for the Democratic presidential nomination. With Barack being assured of the nomination, Michelle was answering more of the inevitable "What kind of First Lady will you be?" questions. A common response was that she would be pretty much the same person that she had been on the campaign trail.

"I'm going to try in all of this, to be honest, hopefully funny, and open, and share important parts of me with people, hopefully in a way that will help them think about

FAREED ZAKARIA ON THE END OF A CONSERVATIVE AGE

Newsweek

He Calls Her His 'Rock.'
The Real Michelle Obama.

$4.95

PHOTOGRAPH BY NIGEL DICKSON

FEBRUARY 25, 2008

newsweek.com

As Barack's chances for winning the bid for the Democratic
nomination increased, so did the public's interest in Michelle. *(Courtesy
of PRNewsFoto/Newsweek)*

their lives and avoid the mistakes we may have made in our lifetime. What you see on the trail is probably who I will be as First Lady, because that's really who I am."

In another interview, Michelle said that she had a lot of ideas, but she had to temper that with some practical considerations.

> I want to bring more kids into the White House of all backgrounds, doing new kinds of internship programs. I mean come on. I'm an idea person. There are tons of things that I can think about doing. But I'm also a practical person. So what can you really accomplish? How much time do you have? What kind of resources do you have? What kind of staff do you have to do it?

Another "what if" question about Michelle becoming the First Lady is if she has any particular agenda regarding women's issues. She's resisted being labeled as a feminist, but she's acknowledged that she's sympathetic with most feminist causes.

"You know, I'm not into labels," she told an interviewer. "So probably if you laid out a feminist agenda, I would probably agree with a large portion of it. I wouldn't identify myself as a feminist just like I probably wouldn't identify myself as a liberal or progressive."

FIRST LADY OF THE NATION

America's preoccupation with first ladies is not new. So far fifty-three women—wives, daughters, daughters-in-law, nieces, and sisters— have held the position, bringing their own unique qualities to the role. Some have been bold: "I know what's best for the President," Florence Harding said of her husband Warren, the twenty-ninth president of the United States. "I put him in the White House." Others have been perceived as meek. Still others, like Laura Bush, wife of George W. Bush, started out quiet but became increasingly active as First Lady. Laura championed the rights of women in Afghanistan and became a leading critic of the military junta ruling Myanmar.

Edith Bolling Galt Wilson, the second wife of President Woodrow Wilson, became a *de facto* president after a stroke left her husband partially paralyzed. Edith strongly opposed allowing the vice-president to assume the powers of the president during her husband's prolonged illness. Instead, she managed

Edith Bolling Galt Wilson helped her husband President Wilson while he was recovering from a stroke. *(Library of Congress)*

many of President Wilson's duties, even decoding secret transmissions after American troops were sent to World War I, and she imposed a self-described

"stewardship"— actions that earned her the names "Secret President" and "First Woman to Run the Government."

Eleanor Roosevelt was another First Lady who played a very public and politically significant role during the administration of her

Eleanor Roosevelt *(Library of Congress)*

husband, Franklin D. Roosevelt. Plain, with bucked teeth that made her voice shrill and high-pitched, Eleanor was called "granny" by her mother, who was ashamed of Eleanor's looks.

As First Lady, Eleanor Roosevelt was not concerned about what type of cuisine was served at the White House, or even how the executive mansion was decorated. Instead, she was passionate about social causes, such as the plight of working women, migrant workers, coal miners, African Americans, and the poor of Appalachia. An active member of the Women's Trade Union League, League of Women Voters, and the NAACP, she famously included

African Americans among her many guests at the White House, in defiance of segregation laws.

Eleanor was also a syndicated columnist and journalist. She became the first wife of a president to hold an all-female press conference, and the first First Lady to deliver a political address before a national convention.

Mamie Eisenhower, on the other hand, kept the lowest profile possible, venturing into the Oval Office only three times during eight years. And Bess Truman never gave an interview as First Lady.

Hillary Clinton had an office in the West Wing and let it be known that she wasn't going to sit home and bake cookies. She was given a formal job by her husband Bill Clinton to reform the health care system; later Hillary became the only First Lady elected to public office—the U.S. Senate—and the first to seek the presidency.

Other first ladies are remembered for their sense of style and fashion, and in some instances, their quirks and unorthodox ways. Mary Todd Lincoln held séances in the White House, and first ladies Florence Harding and Nancy Reagan consulted astrologers. Dolly Madison popularized turbans

Dolly Madison *(Library of Congress)*

for women, while Frances Folsom, wife of President Grover Cleveland, who was nearly three decades her senior, set off a craze with a close-cropped haircut. Women across America began shaving the backs of their necks.

Frances Folsom (*Library of Congress*)

Guitar-playing Julia Gardiner Tyler, second wife of President John Tyler, scandalized her family by appearing in a clothing advertisement. The socialite was accused of being too "regal" and "queenlike;" often she was called "Lady Presidentress" or "Her lovliness."

Julia Gardiner Tyler (*Library of Congress*)

Jacqueline Kennedy, wife of President John F. Kennedy, is remembered for her cultivated tastes in art and fashion. But Jackie did not like the title First Lady. She told her staff not to use it because it sounded like the name of a saddle horse.

The job of First Lady is unpaid and undefined, yet powerful. First ladies bring to the role their own experiences, background, and circumstances, and many have left enduring legacies. In summing up the job, Laura Bush perhaps put it best: "The role of First Lady is whatever the First Lady wants it to be."

Laura Bush

seven
Transition to the White House

On August 25, 2008, Michelle was chosen to deliver a speech on the first night of the Democratic National Convention in Denver, Colorado. It was her first time speaking before such a massive gathering. Her speech was viewed as a vital one. She had the role of presenting a warm portrait of Barack as a man, and convincing voters that he was somebody they could identify with. Michelle also needed to portray herself as warm and nonthreatening, especially in light of the accusations she and her husband had faced of being elitist and out of touch.

After the speech, many reporters and pundits believed that Michelle had succeeded admirably, delivering a moving speech that showed not only what the election meant to the Obama family, but to America as a whole as it moved into the future. Near the end of the speech, Michelle spoke about her daughters, her thoughts on the future, and her and Barack's legacy:

> As I tuck that little girl in and her little sister into bed at night, you see, I think about how, one day, they'll have families of their own and how, one day, they—and your sons and daughters will tell their own children about what we did together in this election. They'll tell them—how this time we listened to our hopes, instead of our fears. How this time—we decided to stop doubting and to start dreaming. How this time, in this great country, where a girl from the South Side of Chicago can go to college and law school, and the son of a single mother from Hawaii can go all the way to the White House that we committed ourselves to building the world as it should be.

The speech was met with massive applause and acclaim.

Despite some early missteps, Michelle proved that she could hold her own, giving speeches that she composed and delivered, most of the time without notes, to crowds large and small. With the Convention behind her, and the general election only weeks away, Michelle showed no signs of tiring or slowing down. She continued to stump in battleground states and make TV appearances on *Larry King Live* and the *Tonight Show*, among others. On the season premiere of the *Ellen DeGeneres Show*, she even danced to Jay-Z's "Dirt Off Your Shoulder," and agreed with the host that her dance moves out-shined those of her husband's, who had appeared on Ellen's show earlier. And when Barack broke off the campaign to visit his ailing grandmother Madelyn Dunham in Honolulu, Michelle delivered the Democratic Party's regular radio address.

After a grueling, almost two-year campaign, November 4 finally arrived. Voters across the country lined up, some

Michelle speaking at the 2008 Democratic National Convention.
(Courtesy of AP Images/Ron Edmonds)

before dawn, to cast their vote in the historic election. Michelle and Barack Obama cast their ballots at 7:36 a.m., central daylight time, at the Beulah Shoesmith Elementary School in Chicago. "I noticed that Michelle took a long time though," Barack joked afterwards. "I had to check to see who she was voting for."

That evening the Obama family gathered with friends and relatives at the Hyatt Regency in Chicago to watch election returns, while more than 100,000 Obama supporters converged on Chicago's Grant Park. Well before midnight major news networks began reporting the results: Senator Barack Obama had defeated John McCain to become the first African American to ascend to the White House.

At Grant Park, Barack Obama acknowledged his accomplishment, and thanked his supporters. But he saved his highest praise for Michelle: "I would not be standing here tonight," he said, "without the unyielding support of my best friend for the last sixteen years, the rock of our family, the love of my life, the nation's next First Lady, Michelle Obama."

With the election over, Michelle wasted no time mapping out plans for her family's transition from Chicago to Washington, DC. First Lady Laura Bush gave Michelle a personal tour of the living quarters in the White House, and the Bush twins, Jenna and Barbara, showed Malia and Natasha around their likely bedrooms.

The Obamas chose Sidwell Friends, a private Quaker school that Chelsea Clinton attended, for their girls. And to seal the sisters' successful transition, Michelle began pressuring her mother, seventy-one-year-old Marian Robinson, to make the move to the White House too. "The girls are going to need her," Michelle said, "as part of their sense of

Michelle stands with Barack, Malia, and Natasha after Barack's victory in the 2008 presidential election. *(Courtesy of AP Images)*

stability." Marian Robinson's presence in the White House would mark the first time in living memory that three generations of a presidential family have settled into the executive mansion.

Forgotten Builders of the Nation's Capital

It is largely forgotten fact of history that slave labor helped build the White House, U.S. Capitol, and several other federal buildings that stand as monuments to freedom and democracy in the nation's capital.

Barack Obama has called slavery America's "original sin," and in his speech "A More Perfect Union," which he gave during the campaign at the Constitution Center in Philadelphia in March 2008, he noted that "I am married to a black American who carries within her the blood of slaves and slaveowners—an inheritance we pass on to our two precious daughters."

Six-hundred fifty laborers spent eight years (1792-1800) working on the White House and Capitol buildings, including four hundred slaves and fifty free blacks. These laborers cut trees, baked bricks, hauled stone, poured concrete, cleared ground, and worked in quarries, among other backbreaking tasks.

In 2000, a TV reporter searching records at the National Archives for the two-hundredth anniversary of the White House unearthed pay stubs to slave owners for lease of their slaves. The slave owners

A 1817 painting of the White House. In 2000, a reporter discovered pay slips to slave owners for use of their slaves. *(Library of Congress)*

received $5 a month from the government for each of their slaves.

Also found at the National Archives were wage rolls, listing the name of the slave, the plantation, the wages paid, and the slave owner, who signed the rolls as receipt of payment. A "Carpenter's Roll" from May 1795, for example, lists five slaves, "Tom, Peter, Ben, Harry [and] Daniel"—three of the five were owned by White House architect James Hoban. Another document reads: "Please pay to John Hurie the balance due for the hire of Negro Emanual for the year 1974."

Besides slaves and free blacks, German, Scot-Irish, and Italian immigrants, many of whom were not yet citizens, worked on the building projects. Many of the white Europeans were skilled laborers—stone masons and carpenters—and they earned between $4.65 and $10.50 a week. Together, these men—free and enslaved—built the executive mansion, Capitol and Treasury Department buildings, and the city streets laid out by city planner Pierre L'Enfant. Slave laborers also devised a method to cast and hoist the bronze statue called *Freedom* to its pinnacle atop the Capitol. The statue stands nineteen and a half-feet tall and weighs 15,000 pounds.

In 2005, a bipartisan group of lawmakers gave a task force of politicians and historians the job of coming up with a fitting memorial to the nameless slaves who helped carry out George Washington's vision for the nation's capital city. But so far nothing much has come of the effort, other than suggested tours, exhibits, and commemorative plagues to be placed in the Capitol. This could change though, with an African American family in the White House.

To her admirers, Michelle Obama is the idealized version of what a First Lady should be—intensely loyal, stylish, intelligent, poised, and always supportive. To her detractors she's seen as strident, overly critical, too liberal, and too opinionated.

Michelle Obama's life is perhaps best summed up in her own words on the campaign trail.

"I'm not supposed to be standing here. I'm a statistical oddity. Black girl, brought upon the South Side of Chicago. Was I supposed to go Princeton? No . . . They said that maybe Harvard Law was too much for me to reach for. But I went and I did fine. And I'm certainly not supposed to be standing here."

Timeline

1964   Born in Chicago, Illinois, on January 17, 1964.

1981   Graduates from Whitney M. Young High
       School in Chicago.

1985   Graduates from Princeton University with B.A.
       degree in sociology.

1988   Graduates from Harvard University Law School;
       goes to work for Chicago law firm Sidley Austin;
       meets Barack Obama.

1991   Father, Fraser Robinson, dies; goes to work as
       assistant to Chicago mayor Richard M. Daly.

1992   Marries Barack Obama.

1993   Founds Public Allies Chicago which provides
       young adults with leadership training for careers in
       public service.

1996   Becomes assistant dean of Student Services at the
       University of Chicago.

1999   Daughter, Malia, is born.

2002   Begins working for the University of Chicago
        Hospitals; daughter, Natasha, is born.

2006   Named to *Essence* magazine's list of "25 of the
        World's Most Inspiring Women."

2007   Named to "The Harvard 100" as one of the
        University's most influential alumni.

2008   Delivers speech at Democratic National Convention;
        becomes First Lady of the United States when Barack
        is elected president.

Sources

CHAPTER ONE: From the South Side to Harvard

p. 11, "My father loved educating . . ." Michelle Obama, "Voting For A World That Should Be," *Chronicle* (Winston-Salem, NC), August 21, 2008.

p. 12, "When we vote, we don't . . ." Ibid.

p. 13, "would practice . . ." Karen Springen, "First Lady in Waiting," Chicagomag.com, October 2004, http://www.chicagomag.com/Chicago Magazine/October-2004/First-Lady-in-Waiting/.

p. 13-14, "the smallest room . . ." Rosalind Rossi, "The Woman Behind Obama," *Chicago Sun-Times*, January 20, 2007, http://www.suntimes.com/news/metro/221458,CST- NWS-mich21.article.

p. 14, "If I had to . . ." Lauren Collins, "The Other Obama," *New Yorker*, March 10, 2008, 92.

p. 14, "yeah, she's got a . . ." Susan Saulny, "Michelle Obama Thrives in Campaign Trenches," *New York Times*, February 14, 2008,http://www.nytimes.com/2008/02/14/us/politics/14michelle.html?pagewanted=3&_r=1.

p. 14, "we alternated washing . . ." Rossi, "The Woman Behind Obama," *Chicago Sun-Times*.

p. 15, "More important, even . . ." Collins, "The Other Obama."

p. 15, "I'm disappointed," Richard Wolffe, "Barack's Rock," *Newsweek*, February 25, 2008, 30.

p. 15, "You never wanted to . . ." Ibid.

p. 15, "She was the secretary . . ." Sharon Churcher, "Mrs. O: The Truth About Michelle Obama's 'working class' Credentials," *Daily Mail* (UK), February 23, 2008, Mailonline.com,http://www.dailymail.co.uk/femail/article-517824/Mrs-O-The truth-Michelle-Obamas-working-class-credentials.html.

p. 16, "We had very hardworking . . ." Liz Halloran, "Q&A Michelle Obama: From the soccer field to the stump," *U.S. News & World Report*, February 1, 2008.

p. 16, "That's the best way . . ." Collins, "The Other Obama," 92.

p. 16-17, "She used to have . . ." Wolffe, "Barack's Rock," 30.

p. 19, "A black kid . . ." Ibid.

p. 20, "I was horrified . . ." Brian Feagans, "Georgian recalls rooming with Michelle Obama," *Atlanta Journal-Constitution*, April 13, 2008, http://www.ajc.com/news/content/news/stories/2008/04/12/roommate_0413.html.

p. 20, "Michelle's always been . . ." Collins, "The Other Obama," 90.

p. 20, "a very . . ." Ibid., 92.

p. 21, "We weren't sure . . ." Wolffe, "Barack's Rock," 30.

p. 22, "Unfortunately, there are . . ." Collins, "The Other Obama," 93.

p. 22, "My experiences at Princeton . . ." Michelle LaVaughn Robinson, "Princeton-Educated Blacks and the Black Community" (master's thesis, Princeton University), 2.

p. 22, "She didn't talk . . ." Wolffe, "Barack's Rock," 31.

p. 23, "When [Barack Obama] spoke . . ." Ibid.

CHAPTER TWO: "This Guy Is Different"

p. 24, "I was skeptical . . ." Lynn Norment, "The Hottest Couple in America," *Ebony*, February 2007, 54.

p. 24, "First, he was more . . ." Ibid.

p. 25, "I remember that she . . ." Barack Obama, *The Audacity of Hope* (New York: Crown Publishers, 2006), 328.

p. 25, "She knew how to laugh . . ." Ibid., 329.

p. 26, "we went out to lunch . . ." Norment, "The Hottest Couple in America," 54.

p. 27, "the world as it is . . ." Wolffe, "Barack's Rock," 31.

p. 27, "I was like . . ." Ibid.

p. 27, "Not to see . . ." Melinda Henneberger, "The Obama Marriage," *Slate*, October 26, 2007, http://www.slate.com/id/2176683/pagenum/all/.

p. 27, "no personality flaws . . ." Ibid.

p. 28, "It wasn't until I met . . ." Obama, *The Audacity of Hope*, 330.

p. 29, "stirred a longing for . . ." Ibid., 330-331.

p. 31, "I'm delighted for Craig . . ." Official site of Brown University Athletics, "Craig Robinson Steps Down As Brown Basketball Coach; Named Head Coach At Oregon State," *brownbears.cstv.com*, April 7, 2008, http://brownbears.cstv.com/sports/m-baskbl/spec-rel/040708aaa.html.

p. 31, "The first thing I was . . ." Wolffe, "Barack's Rock," 31.

p. 32, "Before I met Michelle . . ." David Mendell, *Obama: From Promise to Power* (New York: Armistad, 2007), 94.

p. 32, "I realized that . . ." Ibid., 332.

p. 32, "We would have this . . ." Collins, "The Other Obama," 93.

p. 33, "That kind of shuts . . ." Scott Fornek, "Michelle Obama: 'He swept me off my feet,'" *Chicago Sun-Times*, October 3, 2007.

p. 33, "I don't think . . ." Ibid.

p. 33, "I told him . . ." Mendell, *Obama: From Promise to Power*, 99.

CHAPTER THREE: Serving the Public

p. 36, "I started thinking . . ." Wolffe, "Barack's Rock," 31.

p. 38, "I came into our marriage . . ." Leslie Bennetts, "First Lady in Waiting," *Vanity Fair*, December 2007.

p. 38, "For the first few years . . ." Obama, *The Audacity of Hope*, 338.

p. 38-39, "There are times . . ." Mendell, *Obama: From Promise to Power*, 103-104.

p. 39, "What I notice . . ." Ibid., 104.

p. 42, "I said, 'I married you . . .'" Joy Bennett Kinnon, "Michelle Obama Not Just The Senator's Wife," *Ebony*, March 2006, 62.

p. 44, "Michelle put up no pretense . . ." Obama, *The Audacity of Hope*, 340.

p. 44, "no matter how much . . ." Ibid., 340-341.

p. 46, "I'm angered, frankly, .." Mendell, *Obama: From Promise to Power*, 136.

CHAPTER FOUR: Mounting Pressures

p. 49, "I was broke . . ." Mendell, *Obama: From Promise to Power*, 144.

p. 49, "I put Michelle . . ." Ibid., 150.

p. 50, "The big issue . . ." Ibid., 151.

p. 51, "What I told Michelle . . ." Ibid., 152.

p. 51, "Ultimately I capitulated . . ." Ibid..

p. xx, "We had known Barack and Michelle . . ." Ibid., 155-156.

p. 52, "Over the last few . . ." Krista Lewin, "Obama brings husband's campaign to Coles County," *Journal Gazette Times-Courier* (Mattoon, IL), http://www.jgtc. com/articles/2004/06/28/news/news03.prt.

p. 56, "We brought her . . ." Mendell, *Obama: From Promise to Power*, 278.

p. 56, "To break the tension . . ." Michelle Obama, e-mail message to author, July 29, 2008.

p. 56, "fabulous speech," Mendell, *Obama: From Promise to Power*, 285.

p. 56, "I just wish . . ." Martin Dupuis and Keith Boeckelamn, *Barack Obama, The New Face of American Politics* (Westport, Ct.: Praeger Publishers, 2008), 31.

p. 60, "This was supposed to be . . ." Mendell, *Obama: From Promise to Power*, 287.

p. 60, "I understand that you have to . . ." Ibid., 293.

CHAPTER FIVE: Balancing Family and Politics

p. 62, "Daddy are you going . . ." Mendell, *Obama From Promise to Power*, 303.

p. 66, "Our future is making . . ." Kinnon, "Michelle Obama Not Just The Senator's Wife," *Ebony*, March 2006, 61.

p. 66, "I still go to Target . . ." Scott Helman, "Michelle Obama revels in family role," *Boston Globe*, October 28, 2007.

p. 66, "People ask how . . ." Kinnon, "Michelle Obama Not Just The Senator's Wife."

p. 67, "Barack and I joked . . ." Mendell, *Obama: From Promise to Power*, 373-374.

p. 68, "I and my wife . . ." Jeff Koinange, "Screaming Crowds welcome U.S. senator 'home,' " *CNN.com*, August 27, 2006, http://www.cnn.com/2006/WORLD/africa/08/26/kenya.obama/index.html.

p. 70, "If Barack really wants . . ." Ibid., 380.

p. 70-71, "I know that I haven't . . ." Jake Tapper and Katie Hinman, "Obama Declares His Candidacy," http://www.abcnews.com, February 10, 2007.

CHAPTER SIX: On The Campaign Trail

p. 72, "I've never participated . . ." Wolffe, "Barack's Rock," *Newsweek*, February 25, 2008, 26.

p. 72, "Since then, the role of . . ." "When political spouses join the fray, they're fair game," *USA Today*, May 20, 2008.

p. 74, "As my campaign commitments . . ." Greg Hinz, "Michelle Obama Leaves TreeHouse," *Chicagobusiness.com*, May 22, 2007, http://www.chicagobusiness.com/cgi-bin/news.pl?id=25090.

p. 74, "People in this country are . . ." Mosheh Oinounou and Bonney Kapp, "Michelle Obama Takes Heat for Saying She's 'Proud of My Country' For the First Time," FOXNews.com, February 19, 2008, http://www.foxnews.com/politics/elections/2008/02/19/michelle-obama-takes-heat-for-saying-shes-proud-of-my-country-for-the-first-time/.

p. 74, "I don't know about you . . ." David Mattingly,

"Michelle Obama likely target of conservative attacks," *CNN.com*, June 12, 2008, http://www.cnn.com/2008/ POLITICS/06/12/michelle.obama.

p. 75, "I think that she . . ." Molly Riley, "First lady defends Hillary Clinton, Michelle Obama," *USA Today*, June 9, 2008.

p. 75, "I've had to clarify . . ." Jill Lawrence, "I don't want to be a distraction," *USA Today*, June 30, 2008. 1A.

p. 75, "What she meant . . . "Obama Defends Wife over 'Pride' Remarks," Huffingtonpost.com, February 19, 2008, http://www.huffingtonpost.com/2008/02/20/ obama-defends-wife-over-_n_87566.html.

p. 76, "You are amazed sometimes . . ." Michael Powell and Jodi Kantor, "After Attacks, Michelle Obama Looks for a New Introduction, *New York Times*, June 18, 2008.

p. 76, "If somebody has evidence . . ." Scott Helman, "Obama takes to the Web to disprove stack of lies," *Sarasota Herald-Tribune*, June 13, 2008.

p. 76-77, "It is possible that . . ." Robinson, "Princeton-Educated Blacks and the Black Community," 59-60.

p. 77, "Blacks must join . . ." "Hannity Repeatedly distorts Passage in Michelle Obama's Senior Thesis to Suggest Alumni Views on Race Are Her Own," Media Matters for America, February 26, 2008, http://mediamatters. org/items/200802290007.

p. 79, "It puts the woman . . ." Scott Helman, "Michelle Obama revels in family role," *Boston Globe*, October 28, 2007.

p. 80, "the same old thing . . ." Toby Harnden, "Michelle Obama launches attack on Clinton," Telegraph (UK), January 19, 2008.

p. 80-81, "I'm going to try . . ." Leslie Bennets, "First Lady in Waiting," *Vanity Fair*, December 2007.

p. 82, "I want to bring . . ." Richard Wolffe, "Finding Her Way: Michelle is Learning How to Be a Candidate's Wife," *Newsweek*, February 25, 2008, http://www.newsweek.com/id/112775.

p. 82, "You know I'm not that into . . ." Ann E, Kornblut, "Michelle Obama's Career Timeout," *Washington Post*, May 11, 2007.

p. 83, "I know what's best . . ." Florence Harding, National First Ladies' Library, http://www.firstladies.org/biographies/firstladies.aspx?biography=30.

p. 84, "stewardship," Edith Bolling Galt Wilson, National First Ladies' Library, http://www.firstladies.org/biographies/firstladies.aspx?biography=29.

p. 84, "granny," "Eleanor Roosevelt," American Experience, *PBS.org*, http://www.pbs.org/wgbh/amex/eleanor/filmmore/transcript/transcript1.html.

p. 86, "regal . . . Her lovliness," Julia Gardiner Tyler, National First Ladies' Library, http://www.firstladies.org/biographies/firstladies.aspx?biography=11.

p. 87, "The role of First Lady . . ." Laura Bush, National First Ladies' Library, http://www.firstladies.org/biographies/.

CHAPTER SEVEN: Transition to the White House

p. 89, "As I tuck that little girl . . ." Michelle Obama, "Remarks at DNC Transcript," *New York Times*, August 25, 2008.

p. 91, "I noticed that Michelle . . ." Robert Barnes and Michael D. Shear, "Obama Makes History," *Washington Post*, November 5, 2008.

p. 91, "I would not be standing here . . ." "Barack
  Obama's Victory Speech," *New York Times*, November
  5,2008,http://edition.cnncom/2008/POLITICS/11/04/
  obama.transcript/.

p. 91-92, "The girls are going to need . . ." Richard Wolffe,
  "Michelle, On The Move," *Newsweek,* November 5,
  2008, http://www.newsweek.com/id/167813.

p. 93, "I am married . . ." Barack Obama, "A More
  Perfect Union," transcript of speech given March
  18, 2008, http://www.npr.org/templates/story/story.
  php?storyId=88478467.

p. 94, "Please pay to John . . ." William Reed, "Slaves
  helped build White House and Capitol," Final Call,
  August 13, 2002, http://www.finalcall.com/perspectives/
  slaves08-13-2002.htm.

p. 95, "I'm not supposed to be standing here." Richard
  Wolffe, "Barack's Rock," *Newsweek*, February 25, 2008.

Bibliography

Bennetts, Leslie. "First Lady in Waiting." *Vanity Fair*, December 2007.

Cottle, Michelle. "Wife Lessons: Why Michelle Obama is no Hillary Clinton." *New Republic*, March 26, 2008.

Douglass, Linda. "A Q&A with Michelle Obama." *National Journal*, October 26, 2007.

Dupuis, Martin, and Keith Boeckelman. *Barack Obama, the New Face of American Politics.* Westport, Ct.: Praeger Publishers, 2008.

Fornek, Scott. "Michelle Obama: 'He swept me off my feet.'" *Chicago Sun-Times*, October 3, 2007.

Gibbs, Nancy, and Jay Newton-Small. "The War Over Michelle." *Time*, June 2, 2008.

Hackney, Suzette. "Michelle Obama shares dreams." *Detroit Free Press*, July 10, 2008.

Halloran, Liz. "Q&A: Michelle Obama: From the soccer field to the stump." *U.S. News and World Report*, February 1, 2008.

Helman, Scott. "Michelle Obama revels in family role." *Boston Globe*, October 28, 2007.

Kantor, Jodi, and Jeff Zeleny. "Michelle Obama Adds New Role to Balancing Act." *New York Times*, May 18, 2007.

Kelley, Raina. "A Real Wife, in a Real Marriage." *Newsweek*, February 25, 2008.

Kinnon, Joy Bennett. "Michelle Obama: Not Just The Senator's Wife." *Ebony*, March 2006.

Koppelman, Alex. "Get ready for the attacks on Michelle Obama." *Salon*, June 11, 2008. http://www.salon.com/politics/war_room/2008/06/11/michelle_obama_fair/index.html

Kornblut, Anne E. "Michelle Obama's Career Timeout." *Washington Post*, May 11, 2007.

Lawrence, Jill. "I don't want to be a distraction." *USA Today*, June 30, 2008.

Lewin, Krista. "Obama brings husband's campaign to Coles County." *Journal-Gazette Times-courier*, June 28, 2004.

Macintyre, Ben. "Michelle Obama – asset or liability?" (London) *Times*, May 8, 2008.

Mattingly, David. "Michelle Obama Likely Target of Conservatives." *CNN.com*, June 12, 2008. http://www.cnn.com/2008/POLITICS/06/12/michelle.obama/.

Norment, Lynn. "The Hottest Couple in America." *Ebony*, February 2007.

Obama, Barack. *The Audacity of Hope: Thoughts on Reclaiming the American Dream*. New York: Crown Publishers, 2006.

———. *Dreams from My Father: A Story of Race and Inheritance*. New York: Three Rivers Press, 1995.

Riley, Molly. "First lady defends Hillary Clinton, Michelle Obama." *USA Today*, June 9, 2008.

Rohter, Larry. "Candidates detail personal finances." *Sarasota (Fl.) Herald-Tribune*, June 14, 2008.

Stanley, Alessandra. "Candidate's wife gives TV watchers a new view." *Sarasota (Fl.) Herald-Tribune*, June 19, 2008.

Tapper, Jack, and Katie Hinman. "Obama Declares His Candidacy." *ABC News.com*, February 10, 2007. http://abcnews.go.com/GMA/Politics/story?id=2865196&page=1.

Taylor, Stuart Jr. "Obama's Wife and Their Spiritual Advisor." *National Journal*, April 5, 2008.

Townes, Glenn. "Rev. Wright episode was 'opportunity' to lead, says Michelle Obama." *New York Amsterdam News*, April 17-April 23, 2008.

Westcott, Kathryn. "The new breed of candidate's spouse." *BBC News*, February 14, 2008. http://news.bbc.co.uk/2/hi/americas//207323.stm.

Zeleny, Jeff. "Q&A with Michelle Obama." *Chicago Tribune*, December 24, 2005.

Web sites

http://www.facebook.com/pages/Michelle-Obama/ 22092775577
Michelle Obama's page on Facebook. Viewers of the page can become supporters of Michelle, view photos, and read notes from Michelle. There is also a news-feed of articles about Michelle from other sources.

http://www.politico.com/news/stories/0208/8642.html
Page about Michelle's Princeton thesis, with a link to the full text of the thesis.

http://www.firstladies.org/index.htm
Features brief biographies and images of every First Lady in U.S. history. Also features information about exhibits sponsored by the First Ladies' Library, as well as curriculum and travel information.

http://michelleobamawatch.com/
A blog devoted to documenting all media about Michelle Obama. Articles are linked to, and users can make comments about the articles, and how Michelle is portrayed in them.

Index